# RECORDING AUDIOBOOKS:

How To Record Your Audiobook Narration For Audible, iTunes, & More

**GEORGE SMOLINSKI**

# Disclaimer

All attempts have been made to verify the information contained in this book but the author and publisher do not bear any responsibility for errors or omissions. Any perceived negative connotation of any individual, group, or company is purely unintentional. Furthermore, this book is intended as a guide and as such, any and all responsibility for actions taken upon reading this book lies with the reader alone and not with the author or publisher. Additionally, it is the reader's responsibility alone and not the author's or publisher's to ensure that all applicable laws and regulations for business practice are adhered to. Lastly, I sometimes utilize affiliate links in the content of this book and as such, if you make a purchase through these links, I will gain a small commission. I have personally used each of the services listed in this book, however, and as such I can say that I would recommend them to my closest friend with the same ease that I now recommend them to you. My opinion is not for sale.

Copyright © 2018 by Gutenberg Reloaded

All rights reserved. No part of this publication may be reproduced, distributed, or transmitted in any form or by any means, including photocopying, recording, or other electronic or mechanical methods, without the prior written permission of the publisher, except in the case of brief quotations embodied in critical reviews and certain other noncommercial uses permitted by copyright law.

# Table of Contents

INTRODUCTION ..................................................................... 1

CHAPTER ONE:
Recommended Equipment & Getting Started ................. 7

CHAPTER TWO:
Preparing To Record ........................................................ 13

CHAPTER THREE:
Taking Care Of Your Voice & Making The Most Of Your Vocal Abilities ............................................................................. 23

CHAPTER FOUR:
Recording in GarageBand .............................................. 27

CHAPTER FIVE:
Recording in Audacity .................................................... 35

CHAPTER SIX:
File Storage ..................................................................... 39

CHAPTER SEVEN:
Uploading Your Audiobook to ACX ............................... 43

BONUS CHAPTER:
Audiobook Marketing ..................................................... 51

CONCLUSION .................................................................... 57

# INTRODUCTION

*"When you read a book, the story definitely happens inside your head. When you listen, it seems to happen in a little cloud all around it, like a fuzzy knit cap pulled down over your eyes."*—Robin Sloan

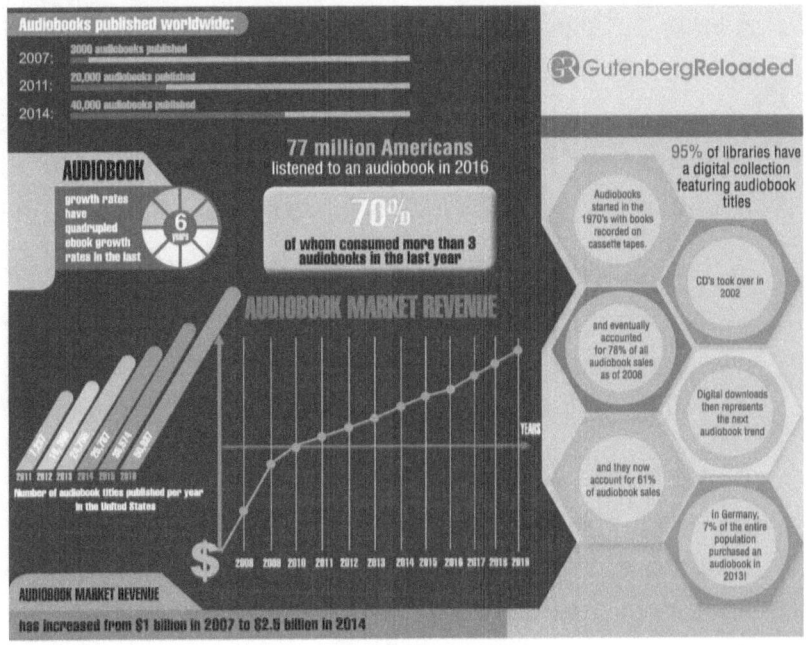

Figure 1.

It's no secret that audio is hot. Take a look at the explosive growth in the podcasting industry and you'll realize that the advent of consuming content via audio is here. Everyone is listening to podcasts or audiobooks on their smartphone while they're working out in the gym, or commuting to work in their car or in the subway. It's an easy way to consume content, and more people are using this form as their preferred way of "reading". Take a look at recent audiobook trends on figure 1.

## Why, then, have audiobook sales skyrocketed?

Here's a list of the top 3 reasons:

1. **Easy To Consume:** almost 100 million Americans drive to work each day, with a total average commute time of over 50 minutes. On average, most novellas are around 40,000 to 50,000 words, and audiobook recordings are read at the rate of about 9,000 words per hour. Think about it: That's one book consumed per week just while driving in the car! Don't forget about listening to audiobooks while grocery shopping, in the gym, walking the dog, doing housework, etc., etc.

2. **Smartphones and tablets:** With the advent of high speed wireless networks across the nation, people can purchase and download audiobooks easily and start listening immediately.

3. **Audio brings your book to life:** A strong subset of readers prefer audiobook content above all other ways of consuming content, and for a good reason: A well-read audiobook brings another dimension to a book. It's the same reason why movie versions of books are so incredibly popular—the book is brought to life. Audio does much of the same, and more and more people are discovering this way of consuming books.

My personal experience with audiobooks has been very positive. I've published numerous books on Audible and every single book has had sales. In fact, my sales have grown with each successive audiobook published, and recently I surpassed 10,000 audiobooks sold. These facts speak to my firm belief that publishing an audiobook on Audible.com provides significant benefits to your publication plans.

Specifically pertaining to publication, having your ebook narrated into an audiobook serves several purposes. First, it helps further your legitimacy. If you are an author that also has an audiobook recorded from your ebook, the average consumer is more likely to consider you as an authority on the subject matter at hand.

Second, there is additional potential to generate revenue from an audiobook. Audible.com has several royalty structures for its audiobooks, and the royalties depend on how the consumer purchases the book – whether it is through their very first purchase on Audible.com or through their established membership. Regardless of the method, the fact remains that this is a viable source of revenue as each audiobook sale will yield at a minimum $1.00 (and that's for the lowest-priced audiobook on Audible—$3.95). Granted, that's a lower royalty rate than many Kindle books, but what Audible offers that Kindle does not is the Audible Bounty Payment. If a consumer purchases your book as their first book on Audible—having signed up for an Audible.com membership—you will receive a $75 bonus along with the royalty payment for that book! This can be a substantial amount of income, and some Audible authors make far more with their bounty payments than their audiobook royalties!

The third reason why you need to have your book recorded as an audiobook is because you need to reach your readers using their preferred method of consuming content. As I stated previously, many people are choosing audio as their preferred way of consuming content and it's a known fact that audiobook aficionados are rabid fans of that medium. In order to broadcast your message with the widest possible net, you need to ensure that you are reaching your customers through their ears as well as their eyes and capture these eager fans.

Here's the short & sweet summary of how you make an audiobook:

**Step 1:** Obtain the RIGHT equipment—a quality microphone, pop screen, and choose a computer program (GarageBand vs Audacity, usually) on which to record

**Step 2:** Set up your equipment in a space that is suitable for recording (read: QUIET) and make sure all your equipment functions correctly

**Step 3:** Record your audio

**Step 4:** Send your audio to an audio engineer for editing

**Step 5:** Modify your cover for ACX standards (they need a square cover instead of the normal rectangle cover you see on Amazon)

**Step 6:** Create your ACX account & enter your bank account and tax information for royalty payments

**Step 7:** Upload your book description, choose a category for your audiobook, upload your audio and cover, and submit to ACX for their review

Step 8: Once approved, market the heck out of your audiobook!

In this book, I'm going to give you all the tools you need to record your own book for the Audiobook Creation Exchange (ACX) and cover every single step above in detail. ACX is the platform on which Audible and iTunes host their audio content, analogous to the Kindle Direct Publishing platform for Kindle eBooks. I'll cover all of the tips and tricks you need to get great sounding audio and then how to upload the files to ACX successfully. I'll also give you some of my best ideas for audiobook marketing, so be sure to read this book to the end!

Now if you learn better by watching videos than by reading, I've got a great option for you: I've put together a course on recording your own audiobook with some extra bonuses in it, located at https://evolvepreneur.club/courses/home/34/recording-audiobooks-course. I go through step by step all you need to record your own audiobook and if you get through the course and are STILL overwhelmed, no sweat. You can credit the cost of the course towards production of an audiobook with one of our voice artists – We have you covered!

The specifics that ACX requires in terms of audio are actually quite simple. ACX is the posting platform for the audio content on Audible.com. I've listed the guidelines below for your reference, or you can go to http://www.acx.com/help/acx-audio-submission-requirements/201456300 and view the audio requirements in detail. After you've reviewed the ACX requirements for audio, you can start your recordings.

CHAPTER ONE:

# RECOMMENDED EQUIPMENT & GETTING STARTED

*"It matters little how much equipment we use;
It matters much that we be masters of all we do use"*
—Sam Abell

Given the fact that an audiobook is almost a must-have in the publishing world, the next logical question is, "How do you do it?" Recording an audiobook can seem intimidating, since you will need to purchase, set up, and learn to use some equipment. You will need to know how to set up your recording software on your computer properly, and have your book cover modified for ACX. But recording an audiobook is not as difficult as it sounds. With a minimal amount of equipment, training, and set up, anyone can record their own audiobook. Let's talk about the steps and equipment that you'll need:

## Equipment:

Needed: Microphone, pop screen, and computer

Optional but nice: Sound treatment to deaden extraneous noise, audio interface

## Microphones

Low end ($52): Audio Technica ATR 2100. This exact microphone is the one that I've personally used with great success; my friend, Dave Barron (who is a professional audio engineer), has given me his stamp of approval this mic. It is a dynamic mic (read: more durable than a condenser mic) and records via USB input into your computer. It has a cardioid (heart-shaped) recording pattern meaning that it records what comes in from the front of the mic and rejects noise from the back of the mic—very nice for recording from just your own voice as the source. It is extremely affordable at only a hair over $50 and widely used by audiobook voice artists.

Mid range ($109): Blue Yeti. This is a condenser mic, has a USB input into your computer, and its a "mic of mics", meaning it can record from many different directions of your choosing. An added benefit is that gain control is on mic itself so you don't adjust input volume on the computer—this results in a slightly higher quality (and less "hissy") recording. The Blue Yeti also has a headphone jack, a mute button (nice for interviews), and cardioid, omnidirectional, and bidirectional settings. The base (not Pro) model is USB-only however.

High End ($230): Rode NT-1A. This is a condenser, cardioid mic, and is XLR ONLY. This means you'll need an audio interface to power the mic, convert the audio input to digital, and then output the signal via USB to your computer as you cannot plug this mic directly into your computer. That said, it's an amazing mic and the quality cannot be beat!

## Pop Screen:

Its highly recommended to use a pop screen[1], which is simply a piece of thin nylon that is stretched across a frame so that it makes the "P" sound that you produce with your lips (known in the business as "plosives") much more muted. Without a pop screen, your "P" will really pop, and this can be very distracting to the listener. This ten dollar investment is well worth the money in terms of improving the audio quality of your recordings. Place it about 2-3 inches away from your microphone.

## Optional Equipment: Audio Interface

If you input your audio directly into your computer, you're relying on your computer's audio card to accept that signal and process it. Typically computer audio cards are not great but for audiobooks they will pass muster. But, if you want a really superb recording, you should use an XLR cable (records in analog) and then that goes to an "audio interface" (one reasonably priced option below) that then outputs the signal via USB to your computer. This unit is compatible with both Mac and PC computers.

Focusrite Scarlett 2i2 USB Recording Audio Interface. Its even cooler because it gives you feedback on how hot your audio is with color-coded gain knobs.

Recording Software: Two easy-to-use (and free) programs are available to record audio: GarageBand for Mac and Audacity. Setting

---

[1] http://www.amazon.com/gp/product/B008AOH1O6/

up Audiacity GarageBand to appropriately record audio is not tremendously difficult to do. Later on, I provide guidance on how to properly set up these platforms for recording your audiobook and **there are step by step instructions available on our Gutenberg Reloaded YouTube channel, located at http://www.youtube.com/c/gutenbergreloadedpublishing** However, note that even if you record using the standards required by ACX, it is also assured that you will need your audio professionally edited in order for it to be accepted onto Audible.com to ensure that the specific spacing, noise levels, etc are all within ACX's strict quality standards.

Audio Editing: Even after you've recorded your audio, you're going to need to edit it to remove any long pauses, coughing or other anomalies in the audio that would not be pleasant for the listener to hear. To properly edit your audio, you have two options. The first option is to do it yourself. I'll be honest—this could easily be the most frustrating thing you've ever done as sound engineering is an art and a science. People study for years to learn how to do it correctly! The other far simpler option is to simply outsource the audio engineering. I've used audio engineers from Upwork with great success, and the rates are very reasonable; our company (Gutenberg Reloaded[2]) also offers the option of engineering audio recordings which we've done for numerous authors worldwide with great success. If you're busy and/or you do not want to spend time doing your own editing, I would recommend outsourcing the audio editing as it is a technically challenging process that is best left to professionals.

It's important to remember that when you are recording audio for ACX, you're going to need to record with some specific features. First, there must be a 0.5 second to 1 second pause at the beginning of each

---

[2] http://gutenbergreloaded.com/

individual chapter, your table of contents, your introduction, your conclusion, and your retail audio sample. And then you're going to need a tail pause that is just a dead space – where there is no sound recorded but the recording device is still recording – of 1 second to 5 seconds. This is so that the reader has a pause in between the introduction, the chapters, etc. so that they know that they're moving on to a new section of the audio recording.

You're also going to need to record a retail audio sample for your book. You don't necessarily have to go back and record a new sample. Instead, I recommend choosing a three-minute sample from the introduction or the first chapter of your book that really captures the essence of your manuscript and grabs the reader's attention. This retail audio sample is something that the reader can listen to on Audible.com, in order to decide whether or not they want to download your book. So, this is your chance to really "sell" your book.

One other quick note: Normally, when recording an audiobook, you do NOT record the following sections:

- The table of contents
- The back matter (disclaimer pages, etc.)
- Any sample excerpts from other books; note that most authors simply choose to read in a "If you've liked this book, please visit Audible.com and check out [insert name of book here] as I think you'll really enjoy it!"

This only scratches the surface of the ACX requirements, and again, please familiarize yourself with the ACX audio recording guidelines before you start recording if you decide to do it yourself.

CHAPTER TWO:

# PREPARING TO RECORD

*"Success depends upon previous preparation, and without such preparation there is sure to be failure."*

— Confucius

When preparing to record your audiobook, your first step should be to have a fresh understanding of the material you are about to record. Guy McDowell, a tech blogger, contends that the least- expensive method with which this can be done is re-reading the book with a set of colored pencils at-hand. Use the pencils to color-code pauses, sound effects, or planned changes in voice or tone. This is especially important if your book requires character voices or other shifts in tone, which require heavy vocal inflection. Your listeners cannot read your mind, and therefore vocal consistence is key. Having this annotated beforehand is crucial so that you can truly bring your book to life.

Since you probably want your recording to sound as professional as possible, you should also have a space in which your project will not be muddled by outside sounds. According to Geoffrey Goetz, the best place in any home is a closet. Provided it is large enough to comfortably hold yourself and your recording materials, its smaller space and clothing-lined interior make it the perfect atmosphere for absorbing echoes and other ambient noises that could arise in a larger room.

These elements of preparation should make your recording process smoother, as well as more enjoyable as you will not have as many factors to keep in check as you create your audiobook.

## How Is Our Voice Created?

Let's break down some basic anatomy regarding your voice. Sound comes from air passing over your vocal cords and then the vocal cords vibrate, creating sound. That sound is further modified by our mouth, tongue and nose into human speech. Our chest also helps create deeper bass noises, and all of this comes into play when recording an audiobook. Specifically, the closer you are to the microphone, the greater chance you have of picking up more bass noises from your chest, but you also have a greater chance of picking up "nose noise"—that nasal, flat sound you sometimes hear when people speak. The takeaway lesson? You need to experiment with mic position in order to find the optimal position for your personal voice.

## How Can You Get A Consistent-Sounding Recording?

There are other factors that impact your voice, and you must learn to control as many of these variables as possible in order to obtain a great, consistent-sounding recording. Why? Its simple: AUDIBLE WANTS CONSISTENCY IN THEIR RECORDINGS! Its true: ACX does a specific check during their quality control process to ensure the recorded audio for a book is consistent, and if you control these variables, your audio engineer will have less work to do and there's a greater chance your book will be accepted by ACX.

The first factor to control is the dryness of your mouth and the wetness of your lips. Trust me, if you read aloud for an hour or two, your mouth is going to dry out and so will your lips! That's why keeping a glass of water nearby is crucial and applying lip balm both before and during recordings is important. This will help minimize the "lip smacking" type noises you can sometimes hear on poorly recorded audio.

If you're still having issues with keeping your mouth moist, here's an insider tip from the voice artist industry: Potato chips. That's right, potato chips! Simply by having a few chips on hand to eat while you're pausing between chapters is a great way to keep your mouth in optimal recording condition. The salt from the chips tends to keep your mouth wet, and the oils on the chips themselves act rather like lip balm. Try it out next time you record as it really does work!

The next factor is to control mic position. I'll cover the specific recommendations for mic placement a bit later on, but for now, simply remember that after you experiment a bit, you MUST keep your mic in the same position every time you record. Why? Your body position and recorded sound will vary if your mic position varies by even as little as an inch, and therefore you must be consistent. Some voice artists will even go so far as to place a little piece of masking tape on the floor to mark the position of their chair when they're recording!

The third factor to control is the time of day. Your voice changes throughout the day depending on numerous variables, including ambient humidity and temperature as well as your own emotional state and fatigue level. There are two important takeaway lessons here. First, record at the same time of day each day. Second, listen to the last five minutes of the previous day's recording BEFORE you start the current day's recording. These two tips will help you ensure consistency in your recordings, and that short listening period will also ensure that you refresh yourself with the mood and setting of your book before you begin recording anew.

## Eliminating Ambient Noise

Even with optimal mic placement and use of a cardioid mic (rather than an omnidirectional mic, which picks up sound from all angles), every recording will pick up both sounds that reverberate off of hard surfaces in your recording room as well as ambient noise in the room itself. Complete elimination of these sounds can be extremely difficult, but there are excellent techniques that you can use in order to minimize them and produce a great audio recording.

Simply put, ACX wants your background noise to be silence—no noise at all! This actually makes the process of sound elimination a bit easier, as you have a set goal: zero background noise. First, I'll talk about setting up your recording room properly and later, I'll talk about the actual mic setup to help eliminate extraneous noise.

In the audio world, reverberated sounds or "reverb" should be minimized. Any hard surface will reflect sound, and sound is also reflected at different rates from different hard surfaces in your room. Think about it this way: When you speak, sound emanates from your mouth and reflects off the wall in front of you. It will also reflect off side walls, the ceiling, the floor, and the wall behind you. Since we'll assume that you're not recording in a perfect cube-shaped room with your mouth in the exact middle of the room, you must remember then that sound travels at a constant speed, including the reflected sound waves. Since your mouth is physically closer to some hard surfaces of the room than others, you're getting multiple reflected waves hitting your microphone at different times—it's a mess! So, we must aim to eliminate ALL of these reflected waves in the most efficient and cost-effective way possible.

The first step (and note that this is a step that is optional, not required) is to find a room that's the right size. Typically smaller rooms will induce less reverb, and by using this handy calculator you can input the dimensions of a room and calculate the reverb of any open space or room: http://www.csgnetwork.com/ acousticreverbdelaycalc.html (note: select 125 Hz for a male voice and 250 Hz for a female voice). When you use the calculator, note that the ideal reverb time is 0.4 - 0.6 seconds but definitely less than 1.5 seconds. If your room is between 0.4 and 1.5 seconds, you should be fine, but the closer you get to that 0.4 – 0.6 second range, the better.

The second step—and this is one you should do—is to deaden reflected sound waves by means of acoustic treatments. The acoustic treatment everyone thinks of is the waffle or egg-crate foam that lines the walls of recording studios. This is great for professional studios, but for recording an audiobook, its overkill. However, there are easy acoustic treatments you can do that will dramatically improve the sound of your recording.

First off, record in a carpeted room to minimize sound reflected off the floor. Second, if you can draw curtains over windows (and doors if available), you'll minimize sound reflected off the glass of the door or window. Third, you should place a drape, blanket, or duvet behind you in order to minimize late reflections. A quick aside—assuming you're recording at a desk, sound that emanates from you and hits the wall behind you and then comes back is a late reflection. Sound that emanates from you and hits the wall in front of you (the wall that's closer to you physically) and then comes back is an early reflection. To minimize early reflections, place another drape, blanket, or duvet in front of your mic.

Equipment-wise, barrier curtains work quite well to minimize reflected sounds.

If you do want to use the foam wedgies like a sound studio, these work well, but you should place them mainly around your recording area—you don't need to line your walls with them! https://amzn.to/2qFxZoR

A clothes drying rack works really well to support the recommended duvets or drapes in front and in back of you.

And if you want to go all-out, this mini-recording booth works great! It surrounds your mic and provides great sound absorption: https://amzn.to/2pNcYlv

The other term you should know is "soundproofing". This term is used to describe how we eliminate extraneous noise from the recording, such as fans, electrical noise, etc. I'm going to divide this into ways to reduce noise from your house and the objects in your recording room and then ways to optimize your mic for reducing noise.

The best way to soundproof a room is to spend time in it and simply listen. Our hearing will normally filter out extraneous noise. Think about it. If you live or work next to a busy road, do you hear the cars on the road all day long? Of course not. Your brain filters out those noises, so when you're assessing a room, really listen closely so that you can pick up those noises your brain normally filters out. Some common sources of noise in a room include:

HVAC systems
Smartphones
Washers or dryers
Dishwashers

DVD players
Pets (inside or outside)
Traffic noise
Bathroom fans
Outdoor sprinkler systems

Pretty much anything with a motor or fan produces noise, so be sure you turn EVERYTHING off when you record!

Sometimes, its very difficult to remove the noise from the closest fan: the cooling fan on your computer. I personally use a MacBook Pro, and that has a very quiet cooling fan. However, many computers have louder fans, and the best you can do is to place your computer as far away as possible from your microphone. Most microphones have long cables, so physically positioning your computer far away from the mic is not hard to do. Its also highly recommended that you use a tablet or Kindle device while recording and read your text from that device as it does not have a fan. If you must have your computer close to your mic, this portable laptop stand works quite well and has two very quiet USB-powered fans to keep your laptop cool and silent: https://www.amazon.com/RAINBEAN-Adjustable-Compatible-Ergonomics-Desk-Black/dp/B07QBQ923Y

A few more tips are in order regarding extraneous electrical noises. First, never cross your cables. Always keep your mic cable physically separated from your computer's power cable to minimize any 50 Hz or 60 Hz interference. This interference sounds like a hum or buzz and its very annoying! Second, if you have an XLR cable mic, this filter plugs in-line with the mic cable and eliminates this noise altogether: https://www.amazon.com/Shure-A15HP-High-Pass-Filter/dp/B00075VQRO

Now that you've eliminated the extraneous noises from your recording room, your ready to optimize your mic position to capture the purest recordings possible.

The key with mic positioning is you must experiment. I'll give you some basic concepts here, but please try out different positions and placement so that you can capture the sound you want. Everyone's voice is a bit different!

When you're recording sound, what you want to do is to minimize the signal-to-noise ratio. Even though you've done everything possible to minimize extraneous noise, you're still going to have a tiny bit of noise in there somewhere. However, the closer you are to the mic, the less noise you'll have and more signal will be picked up. As such, its recommended to start your experimenting with your mic set at about 4 inches (7-8 cm) away from your mouth. This should give you a clear, natural tone to your recordings.

If you move a bit closer to the mic, you'll pick up a bit more bass in your recording due to the "proximity effect"—note that this may or may not sound great for your particular recording so again, be sure to experiment. One word of caution—if you're very close to your mic you also may pick up some unwanted noises from your nose in the recording!

If you're far away from the mic, then you'll have to turn up the gain on the mic (or on GarageBand or Audacity on your computer) in order to record your voice. This, in turn, will give you that hissing noise that you hear when you turn the volume up to 11 on your speakers.

RECORDING AUDIOBOOKS

> ## FREE HOME STUDIO SETUP VIDEO
>
> This book is INTERACTIVE - to get free training videos, access to more resources, updates and upgrades to this book when new versions or editions are released visit http://www.recordingaudiobooks.net/bonus1
>
> There you'll find the FIRST of several bonuses I'm including with this book. My first bonus to you is a video I shot of my own recording setup for recording this very book for Audible! Replicate what I did with my setup and you'll get great audio recordings right at home!

Now that you have your equipment set up and ready, let's talk a bit about how to take care of your health and take care of your voice so you can optimize your recordings and ensure they remain rock-solid consistent throughout.

CHAPTER THREE:

# TAKING CARE OF YOUR VOICE & MAKING THE MOST OF YOUR VOCAL ABILITIES

*"Health is not valued till sickness comes"*

—Thomas Fuller

Think back to the last presentation you had to give for new clients or to your boss. Apart from the stress of the presentation itself, do you remember how tired it made you feel to give that presentation? Even if you're reading a book to your children, you know that reading aloud for any extended period of time can be tiring. If you don't take care of yourself and take care of your voice, it can be very difficult to record an entire book; remember that one hour of recording is about 8,000 to 9,000 words, and even shorter novellas usually have about 40,000 words. That's four hours alone of work for a professional voice artist!

Fortunately, there are great strategies you can use to help mitigate any damage to your voice, keep yourself fresh, and help you maintain the consistency you need to complete the task of recording your own audiobook.

First, and most importantly, you need to get appropriate rest! It is a bad idea to get home from work, tired and worn out, and hop right into recording your book. Your fatigue will show in the recording! Think about it: When you're tired at work (or talking with someone on the phone when you're tired), how often do you hear the phrase, "You sound tired"? You definitely don't want that to come across in your recorded audiobook, so ensure you get appropriate rest and if you're exhausted, skipping a day of recording is very reasonable.

The second strategy is to ensure that you warm up your voice appropriately before you start recording. Recording audio can be a physically demanding task on your vocal muscles, and just like you'd warm up before working out in the gym, you need to warm up your vocal muscles before you jump in to an hour of recording. To warm up your voice, first hum as low as you can for five seconds, and repeat that three times. Then say the letters "R", "Q", "E", "Q" (in that order) ten times to stretch out your mouth. Have a couple sips of water to flush out your mouth, and then you're warmed up and ready to start.

The third strategy is to ensure that you listen to the previous day's recording for a few minutes to ensure you're going to capture the tone and mood of the recording. Its just like picking up a book that you're reading: You need to refresh your memory before you start so your recording will be consistent.

The last strategy is to wash your hands. Obviously your hands have little to do with your voice except for one thing: They transmit germs! Especially during the cold and flu season, nothing will keep you from recording longer than having a cold or the flu and washing your hands to prevent the spread of germs is critical. If you try recording while your nose stuffed up, I can virtually guarantee that ACX will reject your recordings, as you sound markedly different when you have a cold than when you are completely healthy. Again, think about how easy it is to pick up whether someone has a cold based on how they talk? You definitely don't want that type of recorded audio in your audiobook!

## Making The Most Of Your Vocal Abilities

Now that you know how to keep your voice healthy, here are strategies for you to get the best possible sound with your voice.

When you're reading your book, you need to make it sound natural. Don't force any moods or tone; make believe you're having a pleasant conversation with someone and that's the tone you should use for the vast majority of your book, especially if it is a non-fiction book. Obviously adding emotion to key parts (and emotional sections of fictional works) is reasonably, but you do not want your book sounding like a children's cartoon. Along those same lines, using arm and hand motions (just like you'd do in a conversation) is also a great strategy to make your reading more natural.

You also don't want your book to sound like one run-on sentence, so be sure to pause at the end of each sentence very briefly and obviously, annunciate your words well. Speaking slowly and confidently helps your voice sound better, and minor variations with the pitch and speed of your narration—again like a normal conversation—will help keep the listener interested.

Lastly, here are a few tips on how to work difficult sections of reading:

1. **Reading lists:** Read out each phrase as it is a short sentence in and of itself (with short pauses at the end of each phrase) and don't just read the list as one long

sentence.

2. **Tough-to-pronounce words:** Look up the proper pronunciation ahead of time, and type the pronunciation into the script itself so that you can read that into your audio recording with ease.
3. **Websites:** Again, in advance think about how you want to read them in and write that into the script. You can either spell out the website and read the entire link or you can simply say "Google [insert search term here] for more information".

CHAPTER FOUR:

# RECORDING IN GARAGEBAND

Today's most popular platforms for recording are GarageBand and Audacity. As you are probably already aware, GarageBand is an application for Mac devices while Audacity functions better with PCs. Both programs are capable of recording quality sound at a reasonable price, however the two possess different interfaces that make their function slightly different. In the next two chapters, you will be given the full details on how to record and edit your audio in each application for optimal sound quality and pace of production.

GarageBand was released by Apple in 2004, and has since set the standard for other music programs. It has also been adapted for iPad, whose popularity has prompted the creation of more portable recording devices like the Apogee MiC. The application is also available for iPhone, and it is therefore possible that you can carry out your editing on a platform that is more compact and convenient.

GarageBand's reasonable price and easy use make it popular with those who are new to recording, as well as with those who do not have access to a high-price professional studio. While it is available for devices other than Mac, the steps below will focus on the application's original format. The program is rather uniform from device to device, and minor differences can often be deciphered through basic trial and error.

**1.** Open GarageBand, and select "Podcast." This will prime the program to record human voices instead of live music or synthesized sounds, which will, in turn, make it easier for you to edit the project after you have left your studio.

**2.** Reduce the tempo from what has been preset. Normally, GarageBand has a default of 120 beats per minute (BPM). Because the application is programmed to record a certain number of "beats," your production time at this tempo is limited to about three hours. A BPM of 40 is typically ideal, and leaves plenty of room for sound effects, pauses, and possible errors.

**3.** Delete the default tracks, named "Male Voice," "Female Voice," and "Jingles." These tracks are not needed, since you are recording your own voice. To do this, select each individual track and choose *Delete* from the drop-down *Tracks* bar.

If layering tracks is necessary due to your desire for background music or special effect sounds, you can add a background track by clicking *New Track*, which is also under the *Tracks* bar. Please note: I do NOT recommend doing this with audiobooks, even for introductions. Adding music adds another layer of complexity to your recordings, and you do run the risk of ACX rejecting the recordings if the music is not in compliance. You've been warned!

**4.** Make sure you are ready to record. Before you begin the long haul, do a test recording that is only a few minutes long. This way, you can identify the sounds of your surrounding recording atmosphere, the quality of your devices, and the potential for errors in your software. Trust me: you don't want to record an entire audiobook only to find that your microphone levels were low the entire time. The earlier you fix these minor snafus, the better. Once everything is running smoothly, you are free to move on to the next step.

**5.** Record your audiobook. As you might have guessed, this is the longest and the most daunting part of the production process. It is, however, necessary; and there are plenty of solutions to making it less strenuous and more valuable. A key tip with the recording process is that you want to start your very first initial recording with about 10 seconds of silence, and then start reading. That will give your audio engineer a "fingerprint" of the baseline audio from which he or she can then work the processing and editing of your files.

Give yourself a copious amount of time to record. You might also want to officially schedule your recording time, for having your mind on your daily duties as well as being in a rush increases the chance for vocal missteps that could prolong the editing period. Hurried speech is also more difficult for the listener to understand, and makes it harder for others to enjoy what you are narrating. As you record, envision that you are reading to your children or your grandchildren, even if they are just inventions of the future. Imagine that they want to hear every word you have to say, and that you want to keep them engaged for the entirety of your tale.

Pay attention to your voice as you record, and try to limit the amount of time you spend recording per day. Any duration that is longer than a few hours puts strain on your vocal cords, which could cause permanent damage to your voice! You should also keep some water at hand, to keep your throat from becoming dry and your voice, raspy. Try to keep your voice at the same pitch and tone during the story for, as was stated above, consistence is integral for holding command of your narration.

While recording may seem like a lot of work, it can also be rewarding as soon as you hear the results!

**6.** Organize your audiobook into chapters. Often, audiobooks are organized into one chapter per audio file, however some books are organized in ways that do not allow for this method. If you do have a book that is without chapters or that has sections that are too long to be recorded as one file, clump the text into smaller portions that are similar in length and topic. Remember, however, that you should not identify these sections as separate chapters if they are not, in the text. When you are finishing your edits, add markers only where chapters are defined, in your book.

**7.** Edit your recording. There are two ways you can do this. The first, called *punch editing*, happens when you edit the audio as you record. This usually takes a longer amount of time than other methods, however it leaves you with little to do once you are finished with your piece. The other, called *straight editing*, is a more traditional method during which you edit only after all recording has been done. It is often the most time-effective, and you are more liable to find and correct inconsistencies that you might not have caught, had you edited each chapter individually. Ultimately, however, the content and organization of your audiobook should be your guide to determine your editing process.

Removing mistakes in GarageBand is relatively simple, and can be done with a few swipes of a mouse. All you have to do is direct your cursor to the beginning of the selection you want to delete and drag it until you have highlighted the entirety of the undesired audio potion. You then delete the highlighted part using the Delete button on your keyboard and, if necessary, close the gap that has been created by the deletion.

Another problem you might run into is white noise, otherwise known as unwanted background noise. Even from the tiny space of a closet, this can happen. To get rid of it, highlight the selection in its entirety and select *Master Track* from the menu. Next, choose *Details* and, after that, *Track Info*. From there, you can click *Compressor* to select from a list of effects you can use to reduce the background noise from your track. Like many of the edits you will make, this is a process of trial and error. Too little compression results in a recording that can be distracting, while too much compression can make your voice sound tinny and artificial.

As you can imagine, recording an audiobook is complex enough, but doing the sound engineering is another beast altogether! I highly recommend finding a solid audio engineer on a platform like oDesk in order to ensure your audiobook is properly engineered to ACX standards.

**8.** Bind your chapters into a full audiobook. This procedure, while simple, cannot be done with GarageBand, alone. The app with which it can be done, called Audiobook Binder, is available for free in the Mac App Store. With this tool, the only thing you need to do is upload your files in the correct order. The app does the rest, to your convenience.

If you don't feel like downloading the Audiobook Binder, there is a way that you can organize your recordings into an audiobook without any additional applications. First, you must export your individual chapter files as MP3s, a process which will be detailed in the next step. Second, you re-upload the materials into GarageBand, manually slide them into place, and add chapter markers between them. These can be found under the *Podcast Track* menu, and placed between each track.

**9.** Export your audiobook. GarageBand files are, by default, in AIFF format. MP3, on the other hand, is still the standard configuration for audiobooks. MP3 files are also easy to burn onto compact disks, and work with almost any media player.

The conversion to MP3 can be done using iTunes, a program with which many Mac users are familiar. You can also make the conversion within GarageBand, if you want to keep with one program.

Conversion in iTunes is the easiest, however it uses slightly more disk space. In GarageBand, select *Send Song to iTunes* from the drop-down *Share* menu. Your song or, in this case, your audiobook, should appear in your iTunes library with its file name. From iTunes, select *Convert Song to MP3* from the *Advanced* menu. An MP3 copy of your file will appear along with the original and, if you have saved the original file to another location, you may delete it from your iTunes library.

While the above is the simpler of two methods, there is another way you can convert your audiobook to MP3 using only the GarageBand application. From the drop-down *Share* menu, select *Export song to disk*. A window will appear, with a menu from which you choose your desired form of encoding. Choose *MP3 Encoding*, and click Export. Since this file will not be saved in iTunes, it is recommended that you save it to your desktop so that it may be found easily.

In the world of audio recording, GarageBand is definitely a hit with independent artists and authors who wish to make a name for themselves in the world of podcasts, audiobooks, and music. Its reasonable price and universal format have set it at the top of the market for digital recording applications, and its consistently positive reputation makes it the go-to for people who want a professional sound without the price of a recording studio.

Unfortunately, GarageBand is not yet available for PCs. There are several similar programs, however, that are both free to download and easy to use.

---

### **FREE GARAGEBAND SETUP VIDEO**

This book is INTERACTIVE - to get free training videos, access to more resources, updates and upgrades to this book when new versions or editions are released visit http://www.recordingaudiobooks.net/bonus2

There you'll find the SECOND of several bonuses I'm including with this book. The second bonus is a step-by-step how-to guide created by our own audio engineer, Sandy that'll show you how to set up GarageBand on your home computer. He takes you right through the steps of setting up GarageBand the right way so that you can get consistent, high quality recordings from the start!

---

CHAPTER FIVE:

# RECORDING IN AUDACITY

Among the applications that are available for PCs, Audacity is consistently ranked as the best and its available for both PC and Mac. Audacity is free to download and easy to install. It also comes with the added bonus of no advertisements and no requests to purchase other materials. Although it comes at no cost, since it is the product of an independent developer makes it unable to function alongside your PC's media program, as GarageBand does with iTunes. You can still play your saved files from your media player, but you cannot import them directly from Audacity.

**1.** Open the application to a new, blank track. Unlike GarageBand, Audacity does not have any specific settings from which you can select for your project. However, you should not worry about the quality: slip-ups are easy to fix and, as long as you are using proper equipment, you will sound just fine. You also do not have to delete pre-existing tracks like you would, in GarageBand.

**2.** Make sure you are ready to record. Check to see that your sample rate is at the highest quality possible, and that your audio feedback is at a level that will not distort the sound. Your audio settings, which can be found in the *Quality* section under the *Preferences* tab, should display a sample rate of about 44.1 kilohertz and a 16-bit sample format. While these settings give rise to large files, note that it is easier to compress, or reduce the clarity of, a large file than it is to pump quality into something that takes up less space, in the beginning.

You should also keep your feedback levels at attention. These are signified by two red-and-green bars above your recording track, the red indicating the levels at input and the green, at output. Your sound will appear distorted if either appears to be too much beyond the middle mark.

**3.** Record your audiobook. The process is no shorter in Audacity than it is in GarageBand, and requires patience and endurance. Remember that taking your time is more important than getting finished, as it lets you really get into what you are reading. Reading more slowly also helps the listener, for your diction is usually clearer and therefore easier to understand. Remember this key tip: start your very first initial recording with about 10 seconds of silence, and then start reading. That will give your audio engineer a "fingerprint" of the baseline audio from which he or she can then work the processing and editing of your files.

Mistakes, since they are bound to happen, can be corrected by pressing the yellow Stop button at the top of the screen. It will pause the recording so you may organize your thoughts before returning to the task. You can do the same thing if you are interrupted by factors outside your control, such as a knock at the door or other noises that might affect the quality of your sound, like children or pets.

**4.** Edit your recording. Depending on whether you decide to do straight editing or punch editing, the duration of the process will be more or less the same as it would be, in GarageBand. To delete portions of unwanted audio, place your cursor at the beginning of the section and drag it until you have completely highlighted the section of which you want to be rid. Then, press the *delete* key on your keyboard or click the *Delete* option from under the *Edit* tab.

In addition to errors in speech or lapses in tone, you might also find that your audio contains unwanted background noise. This can happen even after numerous test recordings; yet it is a simple problem to resolve. To begin removing these distracting sounds from your audio, select a portion in which you are not speaking. Anything that is audible in your silence is a background noise that can be highlighted and removed. You do not have to find a large gap of silence, either: a few seconds will do. Next, select *Noise Removal* from the *Effects* menu. A dialog box will open, in which you will select Get *noise profile*. The box will then close, as the program has recognized the noises you intend to reduce. Finally, select the entirety of your audio and select *Noise Removal* once more. While this can be done more than once, it is suggested that you preview the track before each trial. Too much noise removal can distort your voice, and ruin the parts of the track that you want to remain nice and clear.

Editing your audiobook usually takes two to four hours for every hour of recorded material, so it is important to remain patient. The results will be worth it.

**5.** Create your audiobook. This is something that is easier to do in Audacity than it is, in GarageBand. There is no need for any additional applications, and it is literally as simple as cutting and pasting. Open the files for your chapters in order and select the full length of each, one at a time. Under *Edit*, click on *Copy* to add them to your digital clipboard. Create a new project for your full audiobook, and Paste the files in order from beginning to end. Divide the chapters with markers that can be found under the *Tracks* menu.

**6.** Export your audiobook. Files recorded in Audacity are automatically saved as .aud files, but these can only be played and edited in Audaciy. MP3, as we have already discussed, is a more universal format. Once you have combined your files into one audiobook, select *Export* from under the *File* menu. From there, select *MP3 Files* from the *Save as Type* menu that appears in the dialogue box. As was suggested you do with GarageBand files, you might want to save your project to your desktop so that it might be easily found.

Since its initial release in 2000, Audacity has made a name for itself as one of the most popular free applications on the web. The engineers at Audacity have also made the program available for Mac, bridging the divide between the operating systems to attain its goal of an affordable, yet professional service for all.

---

## FREE AUDACITY SETUP VIDEO

This book is INTERACTIVE - to get free training videos, access to more resources, updates and upgrades to this book when new versions or editions are released visit
http://www.recordingaudiobooks.net/bonus3

There you'll find the THIRD of several bonuses I'm including with this book. The third bonus is a step-by-step how-to guide created by our own audio engineer, Sandy that will show you how to set up Audacity on your home computer. He takes you right through the steps of setting up Audacity the right way so that you can get consistent, high quality recordings from the start!

## CHAPTER SIX:

# FILE STORAGE

*"I have files, I have computer files and, you know, files on paper. But most of it is really in my head. So God help me if anything ever happens to my head!"*

—George R. R. Martin

Scenario: You've just spend the better part of a week recording your book, you're just about done recording the conclusion, and then it happens. The spinning pinwheel of death. Yes, Macs are reliable computers, but the pinwheel of death—analogous to the blue screen of death in Windows—can take all your hard work and destroy it.

Fortunately, there are reliable ways to save your data that I highly recommend you use when you record, and I'll recommend easy- to-use options so that your hard work doesn't disappear. Remember, unlike programs like Microsoft Word, GarageBand and Audacity do not auto-save your work, so remembering to save every single recording after you're done with it is incredibly important!

My personal favorite way to back up data is to use a cloud based solution like Google Drive or Dropbox. Your audio files will take up a fairly significant amount of space, and as such, backing them up to a cloud storage platform will also free up space on your computer's hard drive.

There are four major cloud storage platforms that I would recommend using for audio files: Dropbox, Google Drive, Microsoft OneDrive, and Amazon Cloud Drive. Each of these programs differs slightly in what they offer in terms of ease of use, storage space, security, and ease of file sharing, and as such, in the next few paragraphs I'll review each platform to help you make the best decision for your cloud storage needs.

**Ease of use:** This is where Dropbox is unrivaled, featuring a start- up checklist composed of simple step-by-step explanations of all the service's features. In the same context, Google Drive offers a fairly smart intuitive interface but it's a bit more cumbersome than Dropbox. Amazon Cloud is the least intuitive and OneDrive falls somewhere in the middle between Dropbox and Google Drive.

**Free storage space:** Google Drive and OneDrive provide 15 GB shared between Drive, Gmail, and Photos. Amazon Cloud however offer UNLIMITED storage which you simply can't beat. Obviously this is far greater than the 2 GB offered by Dropbox (which offers the least amount of free storage space).

**Paid storage plans:** Amazon crushes the competition here; they offer unlimited storage for $59.99 per year. Google comes next; with monthly plans (100 gigabytes of storage) beginning at

$1.99. Then comes OneDrive, offering $5 monthly (or $45 yearly) plans. And Dropbox comes at last, with monthly plans beginning from $9.99 (or $99 yearly).

**Ease of sharing:** Dropbox provides quite a bit easier file sharing than

Google Drive, which takes more keystrokes and clicks to share files. Also, Dropbox includes a variety of options for sharing, providing either read-only access or full read-and-write access, but note that this is offered by Google Drive as well, which obviously enhances collaboration. Amazon Cloud offers sharing only via providing a link to the shared item which makes it the least useful for sharing and collaboration. Google Drive makes sharing documents easy especially if you have a Google account, but also adds the ability to share via Facebook and Twitter, although its arguable whether you'd need that feature. OneDrive is fairly easy, but nowhere near the ease of Google Drive sharing.

**Security:** In addition to emailing you to seek verification prior to sharing or changing any of your data, Dropbox and OneDrive also provide even more security through the optional two-factor authentication, which helps largely eliminate many serious security gaps. A similar feature is provided by Google Drive (but you need to sign up for it (don't worry, its free)). Clearly this is a point where Amazon Cloud largely falls short as they have no two factor verification which is becoming the standard base for security online.

Again, using a cloud-based platform to store your audio files is quick and easy and even with the basic plans (except for Dropbox) you'll have plenty of storage for your files. Whatever method you use, again remember to ALWAYS save your files after you're done with each chapter you've recorded so you don't have to re- record your entire book!

CHAPTER SEVEN:

# UPLOADING YOUR AUDIOBOOK TO ACX

If you don't have an account set up with ACX yet, you'll need to do so, and this is an extremely easy process, much like setting up a Kindle Direct Publishing account for Kindle publishing. Take note, however that currently ACX is only accepting submissions from persons in the United States or the United Kingdom.

For folks outside of the US/UK, you can use reship.com to get the required US address. You'll also need to get a US EIN and get a US bank account from payoneer.com to set up your ACX account. However, please note that this book is not legal or business advice! Please consult your attorney for the most up to date and accurate information on setting up these accounts and tax questions!

After you've set up your account, you're ready to start uploading your audio. Remember, even with the best recording, there's a decent chance that you may record your book and submit it to ACX and they'll ask you to modify the recordings, as minor details (i.e. recording in stereo vs mono or having your peaks off in the audio) can have a huge impact on the listener and therefore ACX will ask you to modify your audio. This can occur even with proper audio editing performed on your audio tracks.

ACX has set specific standards for their audio quality so that their listeners can be assured that their audiobooks will all be high quality recordings. ACX publishes their audiobooks to both iTunes and Audible, and as such, quality is incredibly important. The quality control process at ACX is extensive, and its not unusual to have it take up to 10 days for them to review a shorter 10,000 word book. Longer books will take even longer to review. To be safe, estimate about 14 business days as the maximum to review books of any length except during December, when the holiday season means some delays in ACX's quality control check process.

The reason for this lengthy review is again to ensure that any audio on ACX is high quality and consistent. ACX's quality control editors perform a two pass quality check on your submitted audio. First, they listen to your recording to ensure there's no extraneous noises, plosives, background noise, etc, and they also listen to ensure the audio has the same pace and tone throughout the recording. Second, they listen to it again to ensure that the audio sounds like the actual text of the book! Now, if there are minor variances between the written and recorded book that's not a big deal and ACX will still accept your audio. In fact, even the highest quality books that we've recorded will invariably have a few typographical errors, and our voice artists correct these typos on the fly while they record the audio. However, you cannot have a book that is drastically different than the printed or Kindle version of your book on Amazon, as that would obviously be a suboptimal experience for the readers and listeners!

Apart from recording great audio, there are several easy steps you can take to ensure your audio has the greatest chance of being accepted by ACX. Note that when you choose our services—either to have your book recorded by our voice artists or to have your book edited by our audio engineering team—we do all of these things for you automatically. First, ensure that you don't have any outtakes (repeated sentences or sentence fragments) in your recording. Second, ensure that your audio has no extraneous noises in it, and ensure that you have the proper spacing before and after the recorded audio for each chapter. Third, make sure you don't have duplicate files in the chapters you submit. Fourth, ensure that you only have one chapter in each audio file. There are two exceptions to this: If your chapter is more than 120 minutes long, you can split it into two chapters, and if all of your chapters are less than five minutes long, you can simply record one long chapter (this mainly applies to audiobooks for children).

I encourage you to try your hand at recording, but if you want to be sure that your audio will pass ACX's review, take a look at my audiobook recording services[3] on my site at www.gutenbergreloaded.com I endeavor to provide quality audio recordings at a reasonable price, and any recording that my voice artists do for you is guaranteed to pass ACX's review! Our voice artists do fantastic work including different accents (British, etc) and provide professional-quality recording and we send every recording to a sound engineer to prepare it for ACX submission. A point of pride is that our team has a 100% success rate with getting our audio recordings accepted onto ACX, and we've recorded and submitted well over 100 audiobooks to their platform!

If you are recording your book yourself and you've followed the ACX audio quality guidelines carefully, we also offer audio engineering

---

[3] http://gutenbergreloaded.com/products/recording-audiobooks

services. Since every book is a bit different, we compose a customized quotation for every recording. If you'd like us to help engineer your files, simply send us an inquiry as well as your first chapter of audio: contact@gutenbergreloaded.com and we'll quickly send back an estimate for engineering your files.

To publish your book on ACX, you'll to need to modify your ebook cover (your two-dimensional cover) so that it complies with ACX guidelines. You cannot simply take a screenshot or crop out the middle of your cover to make it look like a square cover (ACX requires you to have a square-shaped cover instead of the rectangular cover that you have on amazon.com). Similarly, you should not stretch the existing cover, since the graphics can be significantly distorted; in that case, ACX may reject your cover. So, you have two options with this. You can either attempt the cover modifications yourself (the requirements for the cover art are listed here: https://audible-acx.custhelp.com/app/answers/list/c/3565) or you can outsource the cover modification. This is an easy and affordable task. I recommend using Fiverr for this. Any of its graphic artists can edit your cover art for about five dollars, and that may be a lot easier and less expensive than trying to learn how to modify the cover yourself. Please note that if you pay more than five dollars for this service, especially from Fiverr, then you are probably paying too much.

Now that you've recorded your audio and modified your cover, you're ready to upload your audiobook to ACX. I've had some problems with using ACX on Google Chrome, so I usually use Mozilla Firefox to upload my audio files. To set up an ACX account, you will simply use your Amazon.com account and once you've done so, you're ready to upload your audio files and cover to ACX.

I've created a video to help you out with this process located on my site via http://gutenbergreloaded.com/pages/self-publishing-resources. When you're uploading your files, you will first have to locate your book on Amazon.com. The easy way to do this is to search by either your name or the title of your book, and you'll have to click on that book's link on ACX.com and claim it as yours. You'll first have to claim rights to the book, and then confirm that your book description is what you want it to be (this will be imported from Amazon.com). You'll also have a chance to insert information about reviews of the book. This text box appears at the bottom of the page under the book description box, and provides a great opportunity to take the reviews from your book on Amazon.com and paste them into Audible.com. The reviews from Amazon.com are not imported into ACX; therefore, having this customer review information on Audible is very important. You'll then be taken to a page where you can upload your audio, and that process is quite simple. You simply click on the opening credits, subsequent chapters, closing credits, and retail audio sample, and upload the audio in the appropriate spot. Next, upload your cover art, and then click on "Done". This will send your audiobook to ACX, where it will review the content. ACX will review it for quality and to ensure that it meets its specific guidelines. In about four or five business days you will receive an email back, hopefully stating that your book has met its standards and is being published on Audible. Alternatively, ACX may ask you to revise your audio, at which point they will provide the specific issues with your recording that you or your audio engineer need to correct before resubmission.

> **FREE VIDEO: HOW TO UPLOAD YOUR AUDIOBOOOK TO ACX**
>
> This book is INTERACTIVE - to get free training videos, access to more resources, updates and upgrades to this book when new versions or editions are released visit http://www.recordingaudiobooks.net/bonus4
>
> There you'll find the FOURTH of several bonuses I'm including with this book. The fifth bonus is a step-by-step guide that I've created to guide you through the process of uploading your audiobook to ACX. Of course, if you don't have the time or inclination to upload your book yourself, we can do it for you including category choice, description uploading, and everything else you need to get your book onto
> ACX as quickly as possible. Simply visit http://gutenbergreloaded.com/products/upload-your-audiobook-to-acx-audible for more information.

## Whispersync—Great Idea or Does It Punish Authors?

Two years ago, Amazon and Audible worked together to release the "Whispersync" feature for Kindle eBooks and Audible audiobooks. How Whispersync works is that if someone has purchased the Kindle eBook version of your book, they can then purchase the Audible audiobook at a significantly reduced price. ACX is somewhat secretive about the actual discount pricing, noting that the audiobook is offered to the reader at a price point ranging from $1.99 to $12.99.

However, doing the math with the lowest-priced audiobook ($3.95 on Audible) shows us that you're taking almost a dollar hit per sale with Whispersync. As such, although one could argue that this is beneficial for readers, given the royalty structure on ACX, one could equally argue that Whispersync is bad for authors and audiobook narrators.

The question then arises, "How does Whispersync enrollment work?" ACX notes that their goal is to enroll all eligible books into Whispersync, so if you're not enrolled now, its coming. However, there are some exclusions to Whispersync that may be beneficial for you to review. The following books CANNOT be enrolled in Whispersync:

1. Books that are recorded in the abridged version for audio, but published as unabridged on Kindle (Note that there must be a 97% text-audio congruence rate between the eBook and audiobook to be eligible for Whispersync)
2. Books that have several lines of non-Latin characters, such as text in Japanese, Chinese, Hebrew, etc.

Ultimately, the choice of whether to enroll in Whispersync is up to ACX, but for authors who do not want their books enrolled, leveraging the above strategies could prove helpful.

## Audiobook Pricing

I often am asked how ACX prices their audiobooks, and the simple answer is that price is that price is based on length of your book and remember that 9,000 words is about one hour of audio. As such, the pricing is as follows:

- Under 1 hour: under $7 (usually $3.95)
- 1 – 3 hours: $7 - $10

- 3 – 5 hours: $10 - $20
- 5 –10 hours: $15 - $25
- 10 –20 hours: $20 - $30
- Over 20 hours: $25 - $35

Royalties vary on how your book is actually purchased on Audible (i.e. through a membership, ala carte, etc), and the details are located here: https://www.acx.com/help/what-s-the-deal/200497690

## Free Audiobook Download Codes

After you have received the good news that your audio has cleared ACX's quality assurance monitors, you'll then receive an email (usually about two weeks later) with 25 free promotional codes from ACX. This email will be sent to the same email address that you used for your ACX account, and you are free to distribute these free promotional codes so that anyone with a code can download your book for free. This is a fantastic opportunity to promote your book to friends and family. I recommend that you ask your friends, family members, or colleagues to whom you've given the promotional code for a review of the book. This is a great way to get reviews of your book on Audible. Even if only half of your initial readers respond with a review, having twelve or thirteen reviews on Audible.com is fantastic.

BONUS CHAPTER

# AUDIOBOOK MARKETING

*"Write when drunk.
Edit when sober.
Marketing is the hangover"*
—Ashwin Sanghi

Audiobook marketing is a bit more difficult than marketing a Kindle book, as the price of the audiobook is pre-determined by Audible. However, Audible does give you a pretty valuable tool to market your book: 25 free download codes for your book. These are usually emailed to you about a week after your book is live on Audible. These are powerful tool that I'll talk about here in a minute, but first, let's talk about social proof and selling your audiobook.

It goes without saying that having social proof that YOUR audiobook has value is of utmost importance. Why? Any potential listener will think twice if your book has no reviews or bad reviews, and—assuming you have GREAT audiobook—you need to "show" these listeners that your audiobook holds value. How do you get this social proof?

## Its easy: reviews

Now comes the hard part: actually getting these reviews. One of the best ways to get them, however, is to leverage your existing email list. The best way to do this and get these reviews is to offer a free copy of your audiobook and then ask for an unbiased review of it. You have to be so you do not violate Amazon's terms of service (TOS) but it is not hard to comply with their TOS. Directly from Amazon's TOS:

> "Additionally, you may not provide compensation for a review other than a free copy of the product. If you offer a free product, it must be clear that you are soliciting an unbiased review. The free product must be provided in advance."

Apart from garnering reviews with these free promotional codes, here's a list of free and paid sites where you can post your audiobook to promote it:

Marketing your audiobook is extremely important, and there are more places to post your book available online with each passing month. Here is a current selection of the most popular places to post your book, along with an easy-to-use template for posting in these various groups.

## Places To Post Your Audiobook Online

Free

https://www.goodreads.com/group/show/596-audiobooks

→ Great place to get honest reviews of your audiobook & reach rabid fans of audiobooks

## RECORDING AUDIOBOOKS

https://www.reddit.com/r/audiobooks/

→ On the Reddit forums, this is a place where you can post your book but be aware that Reddit can get nasty; be sure you have a superb audiobook before you post it on Reddit!

https://www.facebook.com/groups/freeaudiobookgiveways/

→ You can post your promotional codes here for free and this group currently has over 2,000 members! You can't post more than three total giveaways for any given book and you can ask people to share the post, etc.

https://www.facebook.com/groups/EverythingAudiobooksE.A.R.S

→ This group is smaller at only 400 members, but its another place you can post promotional codes for your audiobook

https://www.facebook.com/groups/1014732691885069/

→ One more place to post your free promotional codes on Facebook; its small at only 99 members

Paid http://www.audiobookblast.com/authors

→ $10 per book submitted and they guarantee that you'll get 3 review requests for nonfiction titles and 5 review requests for fiction titles

http://audavoxx.com/

→ This is an audiobook newsletter service that is sent out to audiobook listeners. You can have your book listed in the newsletter and its fairly inexpensive ($2 to $6 depending on what you want done). They require you to have at least 4.0 stars for your book's reviews and they only promote general fiction, mystery/thriller, historicals, sci-fi/fantasy, romance, and YA fiction

## Asking For Reviews From Professional Reviewers

Here's a list of places where you can ask for a review of your audiobook. Remember, reviews are incredibly important, so don't be shy in asking for one!

- http://audiobookreviewer.com/
- http://www.audiofilemagazine.com/contact/
- http://audiobookjungle.com/about/review-policy/
- http://audiobookjukebox.squarespace.com/solid-gold-reviewer-program

## Template To Post On Review Sites

Use this template when asking for book reviews—simply copy and paste it!

## Where Is Your Book Located Online?

My book is located on both iTunes and Audible.com and you can leave a review on either platform. Of course, if you want to leave a review on BOTH sites, I'll be forever thankful, but an honest review on either site would be most appreciated!

## Are There Any Elements I Should Include In My Review?

Yes. Please comment on both the content of the book itself as well as the quality and reading style of the narrator. Both of these factors are important for audiobook listeners, and your feedback will give prospective customers a better idea of what the book covers and how it sounds read aloud. Please also include a disclosure in your review stating the following: "In the interest of full disclosure, note that I received a free copy of this product for review purposes"

## What If I Really Hate Your Audiobook?

Although unlikely, PLEASE tell me! I try my utmost to produce quality content and great recordings, so if there are problems with the book, please let me know! I must stress that your review should be 100% honest, but if you have constructive criticism regarding my book, please let me know so I can improve it.

## When Should I Post My Review?

Please post your review once you have completed enough of the audiobook to feel that you can give an honest review of the content and reading style.

## Other Audiobook Marketing Strategies

- Post your Retail Audio Sample on YouTube with your book cover and "Buy It On Audible Today" as the background for the video. Ensure your book's link to Audible is in the video and in the video description on YouTube

- Check out this helpful page for an easy how-to guide on SEO for your YouTube video: http://backlinko.com/how- to-rank-youtube-videos

- Give some of your promotional codes to your narrator (if you hire someone to record your book) and ask them to email the codes out to their followers and ask for reviews of your audiobook

Most effective, however, is to leverage your email list to help gather reviews of your audiobook, and to this end, I've created a cut-and-paste template you can use to send out to your email list, friends, and family in order to ask for reviews without sounding sleazy! This template is available on our Gutenberg Reloaded website, and you can access it here: http://gutenbergreloaded.com/pages/audiobook-review-cut-and- paste-template.

# CONCLUSION

You are now on your way to recording your first audiobook! As you continue to create, your skills will improve and let you record and edit at a more fluid pace. Also, if you get frustrated with your first project, know that you are in good company: it sometimes takes a few tries to find a method that caters to your talents, your time constraints, and your personal creative goals. Ultimately, however, you should find the process fun, rewarding, and, if you decide to release your audiobook, lucrative. Authors who release a quality audiobook alongside their print copies tend to be taken more seriously, and are able to capture a wider audience of people.

Do you think you're ready to be among those ranks? With the tools listed above, you are more than prepared to record and release an audiobook that can stand with those that have been made in a professional studio. It's time to face your fears, fire up your PC, your Mac, or your iPad, and get started.

One final thing: if you have enjoyed this book and found it useful, please leave a review of it on Amazon at https://www.amazon.com/Recording-Audiobooks-Started-Audiobook-Audible/dp/B00WZRPM7M

and thanks!